GOD'S Messages
for My Daughter

Inspired by Faith

God's Messages
Daughter
©Product Concept Mfg., Inc.

Gods Messages for my Daughter
ISBN 0-9843328-6-3

Published by Product Concept Mfg., Inc.
2175 N. Academy Circle #200, Colorado Springs, CO 80909

Scriptures taken from the Holy Bible,
New International Version®, NIV®.
Copyright © 1973, 1978, 1984 by Biblica, Inc.™
Used by permission of Zondervan.
All rights reserved worldwide.
www.zondervan.com

Written and Compiled by Patricia Mitchell
in association with Product Concept Mfg., Inc.

All scripture quotations are from the King James version
of the Bible unless otherwise noted.

Where quotations do not have a credit, the author is unknown.

GOD'S Messages for My Daughter

There is no greater joy to a Mother's heart
than the blessing of her cherished child.
Dear Daughter, every day, I care for you...
think of you... pray for you.

For where your treasure is,
there will your heart be also.

Matthew 6:21

Daughter

ONCE you were
my precious little girl...

NOW you're also
my dearest friend...

ALWAYS and forever,
you are LOVED.

Dear God,

How can I thank You
for blessing my life
with such a wonderful daughter?
She is everything
I have ever dreamed of...
and so much more!
Thank You, Lord,
from the bottom of my heart.
Amen.

THE BLESSING
OF A THANKFUL HEART

When we take time out to count our
blessings, especially the blessing of family
and friends, we cannot help but respond with
humble gratitude. We cannot help but turn to
God, the creator and giver of all good things,
and thank Him for all He has done
and continues to do for us.

Lord, grant me a heart of gratitude and praise.

Amen

I have not stopped giving thanks for you,
remembering you in my prayers.
Ephesians 1:16 NIV

O give thanks unto the LORD;
for he is good.
Psalm 118:1

In every thing give thanks:
for this is the will of God
in Christ Jesus concerning you.
1 Thessalonians 5:18

*"Wise men count their blessings;
fools, their problems."*

---

*He that is mighty hath done to me
great things; and holy is his name.*
Luke 1:49

---

*If the only prayer you say in your entire life
is "Thank you," that will suffice.*
Meister Eckhart

Dear God,
It seems like only yesterday
my daughter was a little girl...
going to school, playing with her friends,
doing the things that little girls do.
And now, she's a woman already...
a woman of strength and compassion,
of vision and ability...
and yet forever,
my dear and delightful daughter.
Amen

THINGS WORTH KEEPING

Some things are worth holding onto!
These are things of value, of meaning,
of significance in our lives. The most
important of these are the truths of Scripture,
for these are what God has given us to guide
us and comfort us at every stage of life.

Let Your truths, Lord, fill my heart and mind.

Amen

The Holy Scriptures are our letters from home.
St. Augustine

———◆◆◆———

Like newborn babies, crave pure spiritual milk,
so that by it you may grow up in your salvation,
now that you have tasted that the Lord is good.
1 Peter 2:2–3 NIV

———◆◆◆———

In his word do I hope.
Psalm 130:5

Let not mercy and truth forsake thee:
bind them about thy neck;
write them upon the table of thine heart.
Proverbs 3:3

I need nothing but God,
and to lose myself in the heart of God.
Margaret Mary Alacoque

Let the word of Christ
dwell in you richly in all wisdom.
Colossians 3:16

Dear God,

My daughter has brought
so much joy to my life,
and now I ask You, Lord,
to shower on her the happiness
that comes only from You.
I pray she finds
true happiness in her life...
and especially, in her heart.
Amen

TRUE HAPPINESS

Happy people are not necessarily those
who have an easy life. In fact, many people
describe themselves as happy, despite their
very challenging circumstances. Genuine
happiness is like that because it's rooted in
faith—faith that God is present
and will see us through any situation.

Let me, Lord, find my happiness in You.

Amen

Growth itself contains the germ of happiness.
Pearl S. Buck

---

*When one door of happiness closes,
another opens; but often we look so long
at the closed door, that we do not see
the one which has opened for us.*
Helen Keller

---

*Rejoice in the Lord always:
and again I say, Rejoice.*
Philippians 4:4

Rejoice, because your names are written in heaven.
Luke 10:20

If you want to be happy, be.
Leo Tolstoy

A happy heart makes the face cheerful.
Proverbs 15:13 NIV

---

*Think of all the beauty that's still left
in and around you and be happy!*
Anne Frank

Dear God,

We all need a few words
of encouragement now and then.
If I can't be the one to reassure
my daughter today, please place
someone in her path to tell her
she has all it takes to do whatever
she sets out to do...and more.

Amen.

GOD'S GOOD PLANS

God has blessed you with unique abilities,
goals, and dreams. He wants you to believe
in yourself, in all He has given to you,
and in His love for you each day. Have faith
in His power and strength, because He will
give you everything you need
to fulfill His good plans for you.

Dear God, my confidence rests in You.

Amen

Wait on the LORD: be of good courage,
and he shall strengthen thine heart.
Psalm 27:14

All things are possible to him that believeth.
Mark 9:23

"Courage is fear that has said its prayers."

Do not throw away your confidence;
it will be richly rewarded.
Hebrews 10: 35 NIV

———◆◆◆———

In thee, O LORD, do I put my trust:
let me never be put to confusion.
Psalm 71:1

———◆◆◆———

If God is for us, who can be against us?
Romans 8:31 NIV

Dear God,

My daughter means so much to me,
much more than she
could ever know.
Keep her safe, I pray,
and guard and protect her
wherever she goes...
but most important of all,
keep her always close to You.
Amen.

POWERFUL PRAYER

What could be more heartwarming
than to know that someone is praying for you?
God has given us the privilege of showing
our love and concern for each other
by taking the needs of our loved ones
to Him in prayer. Use the privilege
of prayer often—
it packs more power than you know.

Lord, I thank and appreciate those who pray for me.

Amen

More things are wrought by prayer
than this world dreams of.
Alfred L. Tennyson

———◆———

Pray in the Spirit on all occasions
with all kinds of prayers and requests.
With this in mind, be alert and always
keep on praying for all the saints.
Ephesians 6:18 NIV

———◆———

"When you make prayer a moment of truth
in your life, the heavens open in response."

The effectual fervent prayer of a righteous man
availeth much.

James 5:16

⸺⸺◆⸺⸺

Pray without ceasing.

1 Thessalonians 5:17

⸺⸺◆⸺⸺

In every thing by prayer and supplication
with thanksgiving let your requests
be made known unto God.

Philippians 4:6

Dear God,

Though my daughter
is no longer a child,
I still want to be involved
in her life.
Help me learn how
to care without prying...
how to let go
while holding her close
in my heart.
Amen

A PARENT'S LOVE

When you care deeply about someone,
you're concerned about every aspect
of his or her life. When you're grown,
however, a parent's concern can come
across as interfering; yet that is not
the parent's intention. Let forgiveness
and understanding look beyond the words,
and see only the depth of love.

*Lord, turn my heart toward forgiveness
and understanding.*

Amen

Be completely humble and gentle;
be patient, bearing with one another in love.
Ephesians 4:2 NIV

He who cannot forgive others breaks the bridge
over which he himself must pass.
George Herbert

Forgive us our debts,
as we forgive our debtors.
Matthew 6:12

*"Resentments are burdens
we don't need to carry."*

---

*A man's wisdom gives him patience;
it is to his glory to overlook an offense.*
Proverbs 19:11 NIV

---

*Be ye kind one to another, tenderhearted,
forgiving one another, even as God
for Christ's sake hath forgiven you.*
Ephesians 4:32

Dear God,

I pray my daughter
never loses her childhood ability
to have fun.
I pray she never grows
too old to giggle
and to appreciate
the funny side of life.
I pray she never
forgets how to laugh.
Amen

LAUGHING MATTERS

To live seriously, learn to laugh.
Heartfelt laughter lightens burdens
and makes any challenge easier to overcome.
It gives refreshment to the spirit and relaxation
to the mind, and it brings a smile
to everyone around you. Laughter is God's
ultimate answer to the serious business of life!

Lighten my heart, Lord, with Your gift of laughter.

Amen

A time to weep, and a time to laugh;
a time to mourn, and a time to dance.
Ecclesiastes 3:4

———◆◆———

Thou hast put gladness in my heart.
Psalm 4:7

———◆◆———

"What soap is to the body,
laughter is to the soul."

A good laugh is sunshine in the house.
William M. Thackeray

These things write we unto you,
that your joy may be full.
1 John 1:4

From sour-faced saints, good Lord, deliver us.
Teresa of Avila

Joy is the holy fire that keeps our purpose warm
and our intelligence aglow.
Helen Keller

Dear God,

My daughter might call them
"ancient history" and wonder why
I mention them, but to me the pictures,
stories, and mementos
of her growing-up years
are among my most
precious memories...
and I thank You, Lord,
for every single one.
Amen

TRUE TREASURES

Think back on the years of your life,
and a flood of memories pour into your mind.
Let God bless you with the ability to learn
from memories that have a lesson to teach,
and to treasure with your whole heart memories
of good times with family and friends...
times of sweetness, joy, and love.

*Lord, let my memories remind me
of Your goodness.*

Amen

While I live will I praise the LORD:
I will sing praises unto my God
while I have any being.
Psalm 146:2

⸻

Remember his marvellous works that he hath done,
his wonders, and the judgments of his mouth.
1 Chronicles 16:12

⸻

I look back on my life like a good day's work;
it was done and I am satisfied with it.
Grandma Moses

"Happy memories of yesterday
are like golden threads woven through
every tomorrow."

The Counselor, the Holy Spirit,
whom the Father will send in my name,
will teach you all things and will remind you
of everything I have said to you.
John 14:26 NIV

Dear God,
 Give my daughter, I pray,
 the wisdom
 to know that true beauty
 comes from within.
 In herself and in others,
 may she value
 over appearance
 integrity and character
 of heart and soul.
 Amen

TRUE BEAUTY

Some people spend huge amounts of money
to buy the products they believe will make
them beautiful. Little do they realize that God
gives genuine beauty to anyone who asks for it,
and it's free! Put on integrity and honesty,
kindness and compassion, joy and love,
and be beautiful forever.

Dear God,
let Your Spirit fill my heart with beauty.

Amen

The fruit of the Spirit is love, joy, peace, longsuffering,
gentleness, goodness, faith, meekness, temperance.
Galatians 5:22–23

Judge not according to the appearance,
but judge righteous judgment.
John 7:24

Favour is deceitful, and beauty is vain:
but a woman that feareth the LORD, she shall be praised.
Proverbs 31:30

Let the beauty of the LORD
our God be upon us.
Psalm 90:17

In all ranks of life the human heart yearns
for the beautiful; and the beautiful things
that God makes are his gift to all alike.
Harriet Beecher Stowe

Beauty is the mark God sets upon virtue.
Ralph Waldo Emerson

Dear God,

In Your goodness,

grant to my daughter

the gift of faith...

faith in herself,

faith in her loved ones,

and most of all,

faith in You and in Your presence

in her life today

and always.

Amen

FAITH

Why is faith important?
Because with faith in yourself,
you can step forward into each new day
with confidence. With faith in your loved ones,
you can lean on their comfort, companionship,
and encouragement. With faith in God,
you can turn to Him in love,
blessed with the knowledge
that you are precious in His sight.

Dear Lord, keep me faithful to You.

Amen

Being justified by faith, we have peace
with God through our Lord Jesus Christ.
Romans 5:1

Faith is a dynamic power
that breaks the chain of routine.
Helen Keller

Behold, the eye of the LORD is upon them
that fear him, upon them that hope in his mercy.
Psalm 33:18

*"Faith is the consciousness of a reservoir
too deep for earthly droughts to run dry."*

---

*Now faith is the substance of things hoped for,
the evidence of things not seen.*
Hebrews 11:1

---

*If ye have faith as a grain of mustard seed,
ye shall say unto this mountain, Remove hence
to yonder place; and it shall remove.*
Matthew 17:20

Dear God,

Ever since she was a child,

my daughter has had

a caring heart.

Thank You, Lord,

for giving her the gift

of being willing

and able to reach out to others

with compassion,

comfort, and love.

Amen

GIFT OF GIVING

To be a giving person, you don't need
to be a wealthy person. Truly giving people
know that the gift of their time and attention can
mean more than anything money could buy.
When you give of yourself, you make a beautiful
difference in the lives of everyone around you.

Lord, let my giving bring love and comfort to others.

Amen

It is in giving oneself that one receives.
Francis of Assisi

Live in harmony with one another;
be sympathetic, love as brothers,
be compassionate and humble.
1 Peter 3:8 NIV

She gives most who gives with joy.
Mother Teressa

God loveth a cheerful giver.
2 Corinthians 9:7

Rings and other jewels are not gifts,
but apologies for gifts. The only gift
is a portion of thyself.
Ralph Waldo Emerson

The noble man makes noble plans,
and by noble deeds he stands.
Isaiah 32:8 NIV

Dear God,

It has been my great joy

to raise my daughter

to know and love You.

As she makes her way

in the world,

let her never turn

from Your Word,

but keep in mind always

what is pleasing to You.

Amen

THE GIFT OF A
GOOD CHALLENGE

Some situations in life challenge our faith,
beliefs, and values. These are the kinds of challenges
that can move us from a simple and childlike
understanding of God, to a firm, deep,
and proven spiritual wisdom. These are the
challenges that offer a lifetime of
spiritual growth and maturity.

Lord, guide me as I meet the challenges before me.

Amen

*Misfortune is never mournful to the soul
that accepts it; for such do always see that
every cloud is an angel's face.*
Lydia M. Child

---

*We glory in tribulations also: knowing that
tribulation worketh patience; and patience,
experience; and experience, hope.*
Romans 5:3–4

---

*In this world you will have trouble.
But take heart! I have overcome the world.*
John 16:33 NIV

His anger endureth but a moment;
in his favour is life: weeping may endure
for a night, but joy cometh in the morning.
Psalm 30:5

There's a tremendous amount to be gained
through what appears to be adversity.
If we don't allow the crisis, these challenges,
to take place, then we remain fixed in life
and never really ripen or mature.
Thomas More

Dear God,
    Only You know what will happen
        in my daughter's life,
        and You are the only
        sure source of advice
        and guidance for her.
    I pray she will turn to You
    in all things, and let Your Spirit
    guide her now and always.
        Amen

GOOD ADVICE

People love to give advice,
and sometimes it's difficult to know
where to put your trust. Let this be your guide:
Does the person's advice come out
of personal experience or special expertise?
Does the advice mesh with your beliefs and values?
And most important of all:
Does it follow God's Word?

Lord, thank You for those
who give good and godly advice.

Amen

A word fitly spoken is like apples of gold
in pictures of silver.

Proverbs 25:11

Who is wise, and he shall understand
these things? prudent, and he shall know them?
for the ways of the LORD are right,
and the just shall walk in them.

Hosea 14:9

Who is wise? He that learns from everyone.

Benjamin Franklin

Nothing gives rest but the
sincere search for truth.
Blaise Pascal

A wise man will hear,
and will increase learning;
and a man of understanding
shall attain unto wise counsels.
Proverbs 1:5

Thou shalt guide me with thy counsel,
and afterward receive me to glory.
Psalm 73:24

Dear God,
In everyone's life,
there comes a time
when we would rather give up
on something rather than
see it through. Grant my daughter,
Lord, the willingness and ability
to stick with worthy goals
so she will know the pleasure
of true accomplishment.
Amen

KEEP GOING

True success rarely comes easily to anyone.
Usually, it takes time to work through challenges,
to gain skills and experience,
to overcome obstacles. It can be hard!
That's why God promises to be
with us and strengthen us. The thrill and pride
of achievement comes only
to those who persevere.

Lord, grant me the strength and willingness to persevere.

Amen

*I know of no more encouraging fact
than the unquestionable ability of man
to elevate his life by conscious endeavor.*
Henry David Thoreau

*We are made partakers of Christ,
if we hold the beginning of our confidence
stedfast unto the end.*
Hebrews 3:14

*"Perseverance is the ability to follow through
on an idea long after the mood has passed."*

He that shall endure unto the end,
the same shall be saved.
Matthew 24:13

Let us not become weary in doing good,
for at the proper time we will reap a harvest
if we do not give up.
Galatians 6:9 NIV

If you wish success in life,
make perseverance your bosom friend.
Joseph Addison

Dear God,
What higher privilege
could anyone possess
than the privilege
of turning to You in prayer?
Grant to my daughter
a heart of prayer...
let her turn to you daily
in boldness and confidence,
knowing You desire to hear
the voices of Your beloved people.
Amen

SWEET SOUNDS

You keep in touch with those you love

by communicating with them.

You keep in touch with God the same way—

by communicating with Him in prayer.

Lift your thoughts to Him...

take your worries to Him...

tell Him how much He means to you.

Let your Lord hear the sweet sound

of your voice every day!

Lord, I lift up my voice to You!

Amen

*Hear my prayer, O God; give ear
to the words of my mouth.*
Psalm 54:2

---

*"Joy and thankfulness are the secret ingredients
to all successful prayer."*

---

*Continue in prayer, and watch in the same
with thanksgiving.*
Colossians 4:2

"When you make prayer a moment of truth in your life, the heavens open in response."

Our prayers should be burning words coming forth from the furnace of a heart filled with love.
Mother Teresa

Seek the LORD while he may be found; call on him while he is near.
Isaiah 55:6 NIV

Dear God,

Sometimes it's not easy

to find our place in the world,

especially during the years

of young adulthood.

So I come to you in prayer,

Lord, to ask that

You would assure

my daughter of your presence

and guidance through all

the stages of her life.

Amen

HERE'S TO YOU!

God gave you unique talents, abilities,

and interests so you could fill a

very special place in the world...

a place only you can fill.

As you try different things and

grow in experience and expertise,

God's plans for you will unfold,

and one day you will thank and praise Him

for His wonderful way with you.

I praise You, Lord, for the gift of my life!

Amen

On the good ground are they,
which in an honest and good heart,
having heard the word, keep it,
and bring forth fruit with patience.
Luke 8:15

Believe, when you are most unhappy,
that there is something for you to do
in the world. So long as you can
sweeten another's pain, life is not in vain.
Helen Keller

No one can make you feel inferior
without your consent.
Eleanor Roosevelt

Life is not easy for any of us. But what of that?
We must have perseverance and above all
confidence in ourselves. We must believe
that we are gifted for something, and that this thing,
at whatever cost, must be attained.
Marie Curie

"For I know the plans I have for you,"
declares the LORD, "plans to prosper you
and not to harm you, plans to give you
hope and a future."
Jeremiah 29:11 NIV

Dear God,

What pleasure
my daughter gives
to me! I'm blessed
to have her in my life,
and now I pray that
she will always know
the joy of having
people around her
who appreciate her
and love her as much as I do.

Amen

LOVING HEARTS

Good friends and family relationships
add so much meaning to life.
They make happy times happier, and they help and
support us through life's troubles and trials.
They are life's angels, these friends and loved ones...
and when you find them, treasure them,
for each loving heart is a gift from God.

Thank You, Lord, for those dearest to my heart.

Amen

"A true friend is the best possession."

My friends are my estate.
Emily Dickinson

Beloved, let us love one another:
for love is of God; and every one that loveth
is born of God, and knoweth God.
1 John 4:7

Blessed is the influence of one true,
loving human soul on another.
George Eliot

Let brotherly love continue.
Hebrews 13:1

To let friendship die away by negligence
and silence is certainly not wise.
It is voluntarily to throw away one of the
greatest comforts of this weary pilgrimage.
Samuel Johnson

We took sweet counsel together,
and walked unto the house of God in company.
Psalm 55:14

Dear God,

My heart nearly bursts with pride
when I think of my daughter.
The things she says and the
things she does bring
so much sunshine
into the lives of others...
and most especially,
into mine! Bless her,
Lord, for all she does
and for all she is.
Amen

BEST PICTURE

You may not realize it, but your conduct
sets an example for others. When you consistently
behave with honesty, integrity, and compassion,
you are showing others how to live
a godly lifestyle, and you influence others
to follow your good example. Sometimes a picture
is worth a thousand words!

Lord, let me set a godly example in the things I do.

Amen

*Thou shalt do that which is right and good
in the sight of the LORD.*
Deuteronomy 6:18

I will behave myself wisely in a perfect way.
Psalm 101:2

---

*Let us preach without preaching,
not by words but by example,
by the catching force, the sympathetic influence
of what we do.*
John Henry Newman (adapted)

Don't let anyone look down on you because you are young, but set an example for the believers in speech, in life, in love, in faith and in purity.
1 Timothy 4:12 NIV

It is no use walking anywhere to preach unless our walking is our preaching.
Francis of Assisi

Example is not the main thing in influencing others. It is the only thing.
Albert Schweitzer

Dear God,

In Your goodness,
grant my daughter
the courage it takes
to adjust to real-life
circumstances.
Help her to willingly
accept those things
she can't control,
and use to the fullest
those things she can.
Amen

GOALS MADE REAL

When we start out in life, we often see

no limits to what we can accomplish.

With time, however, we find certain

obstacles in our path—some we can overcome,

others we cannot. Let God's Spirit

help you discern the difference

between these two kinds of obstacles,

because only then can your spirit soar.

Lord, match my goals to Your will for my life.

Amen

*"Resistance causes pain and lethargy.
It is when we practice acceptance
that new possibilities appear."*

---

*It is the LORD: let him do
what seemeth him good.*
1 Samuel 3:18

---

*Do all things without murmurings
and disputings.*
Philippians 2:14

The will of the Lord be done.
Acts 21:14

Be willing to have it so. Acceptance
of what has happened is the first step
to overcoming the consequences
of any misfortune.
William James

I am not afraid of storms
for I am learning how to sail my ship.
Louisa May Alcott

Dear God,
You are able to make anything—
even challenges and difficulties—
work to the good
of those who love You.
Grant my daughter
faith in You so she will trust
Your good purposes
in all life brings her way.
Amen

THINGS WORK OUT

Believers and non-believers alike face life-
changing disasters and tragedies.
The difference lies, however,
in the way these unfortunate events are seen.
What to the non-believer is cause for despair,
is for the believer a reason to rely
on God's desire and ability to
strengthen, help, and care.

Even when I don't understand,
Lord, let me lean on You.

Amen

Those who know your name will trust in you,
for you, LORD, have never forsaken
those who seek you.
Psalm 9:10 NIV

———✦—✦—✦———

Sorrow is a fruit; God does not allow it
to grow on a branch that is too weak to bear it.
Victor Hugo

———✦—✦—✦———

O taste and see that the LORD is good:
blessed is the man that trusteth in him.
Psalm 34:8

The LORD is good, a strong hold in the day of trouble;
and he knoweth them that trust in him.
Nahum 1:7

It is difficult to make a man miserable
while he feels he is worthy of himself
and claims kindred to the great God who made him.
Abraham Lincoln

We know that all things work together for good
to them that love God, to them who are the called
according to his purpose.
Romans 8:28

Earth has no sorrow that Heaven cannot heal.
Thomas More

Dear God,

Through Jesus' work here on earth,
we have forgiveness of sins.
May my daughter never lose sight
of the forgiveness
she has in Jesus,
and may she find peace
of heart and soul in her readiness
to forgive others.
Amen

PASS IT ON

God invites you to come to Him

for forgiveness, and He promises you

He will grant it. But forgiveness doesn't stop there.

God says, "Pass it on!" Let go of

resentment against those who have hurt you.

Turn toward those who have wronged you,

and forgive them. Forgive completely,

as God has forgiven you.

Lord, teach me how to forgive from the heart.

Amen

As far as the east is from the west,
so far hath he removed our transgressions from us.
Psalm 103:12

There is no condition for forgiveness.
Paul Tillich

"He who forgives ends the quarrel."

Bless them which persecute you: bless,
and curse not.
Romans 12:14

"Forgiveness is not for the forgiven,
but for the sake of the forgiver."

Forbearing one another, and forgiving one another,
if any man have a quarrel against any: even as Christ
forgave you, so also do ye.
Colossians 3:13

"One of the secrets of a long and fruitful life
is to forgive everybody everything every night
before you go to bed."

Dear God,

I long for my daughter
to know the kind of peace
that comes only from
doing the right thing,
regardless of the cost
or consequences.
Keep her, I pray, always ready
to follow Your will
in all her actions and decisions.

Amen

HOW TO SLEEP WELL

We're often tempted to bend the rules.

We want to agree with a superior;

we want to go along with the crowd;

we want to win status or recognition.

It's not always easy to keep a clear conscience!

But by acting with honesty and justice,

we possess peace of mind—

and the blessing of a good night's sleep.

Lord, give me strength to stand up for what's right.

Amen

*The testimony of a conscience is the glory
of the good man; have a good conscience
and thou shalt have gladness.*

Thomas à Kempis

---

*Let us not love in word, neither in tongue;
but in deed and in truth.*

1 John 3:18

---

*My righteousness I hold fast,
and will not let it go:
my heart shall not reproach me
so long as I live.*

Job 27:6

Better is a little with righteousness
than great revenues without right.
Proverbs 16:8

———◆◆◆———

A good conscience is to the soul
what health is to the body; it preserves
constant ease and serenity within us,
and more than countervails
all the calamities and afflictions
which can befall us without.
Joseph Addison

———◆◆◆———

I strive always to keep my conscience clear
before God and man.
Acts 24:16 NIV

Dear God,

Times of joy and times of sorrow

come to each of us.

I do not ask for my

daughter to never know sadness,

but only that she possess

the faith and wisdom

it takes to find contentment

in every season of life.

Amen

CONTENTMENT

Godly contentment is a matter of the spirit.
While you work hard to achieve,
while you look forward to fulfilling your desires,
you rest today at ease with who you are
and what you have. You know all things
are in God's hands, and that where
you are right now is
where you're meant to be.

Lord, grant me the blessing of godly contentment.

Amen

Content is the Philosopher's Stone,
that turns all it touches into gold.
Benjamin Franklin

I have learned, in whatsoever state I am,
therewith to be content.
Philippians 4:11

Everything has its wonders,
even darkness and silence, and I learn,
whatever state I may be in,
therein to be content.
Helen Keller

Be content with such things as ye have:
for he hath said, I will never leave thee,
nor forsake thee.
Hebrews 13:5

A little that a righteous man hath
is better than the riches of many wicked.
Psalm 37:16

No one can be poor that has enough,
nor rich, that covets more than he has.
Seneca

Dear God,

In my role as a parent,

I so often failed to listen to what

my daughter needed...

to say those words

that would have offered her strength

and confidence.

For these times,

I ask forgiveness from You...

and from my dear daughter.

Amen

THE THINGS WE SAY

"Words can never hurt me!"
Even children know the playground boast
is far from true. Words can hurt, and hurt deeply.
Yet, due to carelessness, thoughtlessness,
or even willful intent, hurtful words slip out
of our mouths. God would have each
of us listen to what we say,
hearing with the ears of others.

Lord God,
let the words of my mouth bless those who hear.
Amen

The word once spoken flies beyond recall.
Aesop

If any man offend not in word,
the same is a perfect man, and able also
to bridle the whole body.
James 3:2

Shun profane and vain babblings:
for they will increase unto more ungodliness.
2 Timothy 2:16

Let the words of my mouth,
and the meditation of my heart,
be acceptable in thy sight, O LORD,
my strength, and my redeemer.
Psalm 19:14

Violence of the tongue is very real—
sharper than any knife.
Mother Teresa

All spoke well of him and were amazed
at the gracious words that came from his lips.
Luke 4:22 NIV

Dear God,

Ever since she was very small,

my daughter has had

a loving heart.

Lord, let her never lose

her kind and generous

way with people...

let her never give up

her desire to give...

to help...to bless.

Amen

GENEROSITY OF HEART

Your generous heart shows
in your willingness to give others the
benefit of a doubt. It shows when you
reserve judgment until you know the facts,
and when you explain the actions
of others in the kindest way possible
in keeping with the truth. Let God's Spirit
keep your heart generous toward others.

Bless me, Lord, with true generosity of heart.

Amen

*We should behave to the world
as we wish the world to behave to us.*
Aristotle

*Speaking the truth in love,
may grow up into him in all things,
which is the head, even Christ.*
Ephesians 4:15

*Let none of you imagine evil in your hearts
against his neighbour.*
Zechariah 8:17

Speak up and judge fairly;
defend the rights of the poor and needy.
Proverbs 31:9 NIV

The best portion of a good man's life
is his little, nameless, unremembered
acts of kindness.
William Wordsworth

Thoughtfulness, the kindly regard for others,
is the beginning of holiness.
Mother Teresa

Dear God,
Throughout my life I've found
that when I put You first,
everything else falls into place.
Grant my daughter such love
for You that You will be first
in her heart...
in her mind...
and in her life.
Amen

FIRST THINGS FIRST

Do you want to know what's first
in your life? Look at your daily planner.
Open your checkbook. How you spend
your time and your money is a sure indication
of what you find most important in life!
Let God's Spirit guide you
as you set and maintain
godly priorities each day.

Lord, let me put You first in all things.

Amen

*Thou shalt love the Lord thy God
with all thy heart, and with all thy soul,
and with all thy mind.*
Matthew 22:37

---

*As for me and my house,
we will serve the LORD.*
Joshua 24:15

Trust in the LORD with all thine heart.
Proverbs 3:5

Thou hast made us for thyself, O Lord,
and our hearts are restless
until they find their rest in thee.
St. Augustine

Seek ye first the kingdom of God,
and his righteousness; and all these things
shall be added unto you.
Matthew 6:33

Then are we servants of God,
then are we the disciples of Christ,
when we do what is commanded us
and because it is commanded us.
John Owen

Dear God,

My daughter could never know
how much I value
our continuing relationship.
I'm blessed beyond words
to be a part of her life
now that she's grown!
Thank You, Lord,
for the gift of
my daughter's friendship.
Amen

GOOD CONNECTIONS

God desires for you to form close,
loving, and healthy relationships. These are the
kinds of relationships that sweeten your life,
bring you joy, and increase your confidence.
These relationships allow you to give
and receive love, and become even more
appreciative of the great love God has for you.

Lord, let my relationships reflect Your love.

Amen

Where two or three are gathered together
in my name, there am I in the midst of them.
Matthew 18:20

"You cannot take more from a relationship
than you are willing to put into it."

Can two walk together, except they be agreed?
Amos 3:3

The most empowering relationships
are those in which each partner lifts the other
to a higher possession of their own being.
Teilhard de Chardin

Wishing to be friends is quick work,
but friendship is a slow ripening fruit.
Aristotle

Be ye not unequally yoked together
with unbelievers: for what fellowship hath
righteousness with unrighteousness? and
what communion hath light with darkness?
2 Corinthians 6:14

I am a companion of all them that fear thee,
and of them that keep thy precepts.
Psalm 119:63

Dear God,

I pray for the gift of wisdom—
wisdom for me as the next stages
of life open to me,
and wisdom for my daughter
as she embraces new roles
and responsibilities.
Bless us richly, Lord,
for all wisdom
is from You alone.
Amen

WISE WOMAN

Wisdom is a gift from God,
and has nothing to do with how well
you performed in school or how smart you are.
True wisdom comes to those who earnestly pray for
it and who faithfully seek it in God's Word.
The example of mature Christians, too,
will help you recognize true wisdom.

Lord, help me see, know, and desire true wisdom.

Amen

Happy is the man that findeth wisdom,
and the man that getteth understanding.
Proverbs 3:13

It is characteristic of wisdom
not to do desperate things.
Henry David Thoreau

Who is a wise man and endued
with knowledge among you? let him show out
of a good conversation his works
with meekness of wisdom.
James 3:13

*Who is wise, and he shall understand
these things? prudent, and he shall know them?
for the ways of the LORD are right,
and the just shall walk in them.*

Hosea 14:9

---

*I would have you wise unto that which is good,
and simple concerning evil.*

Romans 16:19

---

*"The truly wise are anonymous;
they do not display wisdom
for the benefit or admiration of others."*

Dear God,

How easily I fall into the habit

of greeting each day

filled with worry and anxiety

over what might happen!

But why? You love my daughter

and You love me

yesterday, today, and forever—

we are secure in Your hands!

Amen

NO-WORRY ZONE

If you start dwelling on bad things
that might happen, worry takes over.
Yet worry is useless—and a sin.
God invites you to remember how well
He has taken care of you in the past
and to trust Him with your future.
Replace worry–time with gratitude–
time, recalling everything
He has done in your life!

Lord, help me banish worry from my thoughts.

Amen

The reason why worry kills more people
than work is that more people
worry than work.
Robert Frost

———◆◆◆———

Consider the lilies how they grow:
they toil not, they spin not; and yet I say
unto you, that Solomon in all his glory
was not arrayed like one of these.
Luke 12:27

———◆◆◆———

Commit to the LORD whatever you do,
and your plans will succeed.
Proverbs 16:3 NIV

*Who of you by worrying can add
a single hour to his life?*
Matthew 6:27 NIV

---

*I am an old man and have known a great many troubles,
but most of them never happened.*
Mark Twain

---

*There is no annoyance so great
as the annoyance which is composed
of many trifling, but continuous worries.*
Francis de Sales

Dear God,

I've found so many of the best things

in my life have happened

without any planning

on my part. May my daughter discover

the blessings that seem to come by

chance, and let her

see each one as

a loving smile from You.

Amen

HAPPY CHANCE

Crowded calendars and busy schedules
leave little time for serendipity—
time to explore, time to see what's new,
time to welcome life's happy surprises.
Today, open your time and your heart
to embrace God's many smiles in your life,
and give thanks to Him for
the abundance of His freely given love.

Lord, thank You for my life's happy surprises.

Amen

This is the day which the LORD hath made;
we will rejoice and be glad in it.
Psalm 118:24

There shall be showers of blessing.
Ezekiel 34:26

The pastures are clothed with flocks;
the valleys also are covered over with corn;
they shout for joy, they also sing.
Psalm 65:13

Happiness lies in the consciousness we have of it.
George Sand

Abundance is scooped from abundance
yet abundance remains.
Anne Sexton

He brought me forth also into a large place;
he delivered me, because he delighted in me.
Psalm 18:19

Not knowing when the dawn will come,
I open every door.
Emily Dickinson

Dear God,

My daughter may not realize it,

but she has the power

to bring the sunshine

of goodness and beauty

into the lives of others.

Grant her, I pray,

the desire always

to shine the light of her love

on all those around her.

Amen

LIGHT OF LOVE

Day to day, you touch the lives of others—
loved ones, friends, neighbors, coworkers,
even strangers. A warm hello, a gentle touch,
a kind word from you just might be
the ray of sunshine that soothes a
broken heart or eases a burdened spirit.
Sometimes sharing God's love
is as easy as a smile.

Lord, keep me lovingly attentive to those around me.

Amen

You are the light of the world.
Matthew 5:14 NIV

———◆◆———

*"A candle never loses anything
when it lights another candle."*

———◆◆———

*I am come a light into the world,
that whosoever believeth on me
should not abide in darkness.*
John 12:46

*I do not believe anyone ever yet
humbly, genuinely, thoroughly gave himself to Christ
without some other finding Christ through him.*
Phillips Brooks

*Let your light so shine before men,
that they may see your good works,
and glorify your Father which is in heaven.*
Matthew 5:16

*Being filled with the fruits of righteousness,
which are by Jesus Christ,
unto the glory and praise of God.*
Philippians 1:11

Dear God,
Grant to my daughter
a long and happy life.
Let her spirit remain
youthful, her enthusiasm fresh,
and her eyes ever open
to the beauty
all around her each day.
Grant to her, Lord,
Your very best.
Amen

FOUNTAIN OF YOUTH

Regardless of age,
there is no substitute for a youthful spirit.
When your spirit stays young,
you are able to embrace life with a sense
of wonder and enthusiasm,
and greet each day with gladness and hope.
Faith, your God–given fountain of youth,
keeps your spirit forever young!

Lord, keep my spirit renewed in You.

Amen

The righteous shall flourish like the palm tree:
he shall grow like a cedar in Lebanon.
Psalm 92:12

None are so old as those
who have outlived enthusiasm.
Henry David Thoreau

The one who sows to please his sinful nature,
from that nature will reap destruction;
the one who sows to please the Spirit,
from the Spirit will reap eternal life.
Galatians 6:8 NIV

For with thee is the fountain of life:
in thy light shall we see light.
Psalm 36:9

———◆◆◆———

"No one keeps up enthusiasm automatically.
Enthusiasm must be nourished with new actions,
new aspirations, new efforts, new vision. It is
your own fault if enthusiasm is gone;
you have failed to feed it."

———◆◆◆———

Exuberance is beauty.
William Blake

———◆◆◆———

Untilled ground, however rich,
will bring forth thistles and thorns;
so also the mind of man.
Thérèse of Lisieux

Dear God,

I hope my daughter knows
how proud I am of her.
More important, though,
I hope she's proud
of herself. I hope she takes time
to smile with the joy of
the little girl she once was...
and to rejoice in the wonderful
woman she has become.
Amen

GODLY PRIDE

Human pride leads to arrogance,
but godly pride recognizes the great things
the Holy Spirit does through God's people.
Godly pride finds joy in being the one
who brings happiness, who helps and comforts,
and who shares God's love with others.
When you see His Spirit
working through you, be proud!

Thank You, Lord, for Your work in me.

Amen

*"To love others, we must first
learn to love ourselves."*

He that glorieth, let him glory in the Lord.
1 Corinthians 1:31

---

*Let us remember that within us
there is a palace of immense magnificence.*
Teresa of Avila

---

*We have this treasure in jars of clay
to show that this all-surpassing power is from God
and not from us.*
2 Corinthians 4:7 NIV

That kind of life is most happy
which affords us the most opportunities
of gaining our own esteem.
Samuel Johnson

I glory in Christ Jesus in my service to God.
I will not venture to speak of anything
except what Christ has accomplished through me.
Romans 15:17–18 NIV

The fruit of righteousness will be peace;
the effect of righteousness
will be quietness and confidence forever.
Isaiah 32:17 NIV

Dear God,

*The older I get, the more quickly
the years and decades pass!
May my daughter
live each day to the fullest!
I pray, Lord, that
she will even now,
while she is young,
treasure the precious gift
of her years.
Amen*

SENSE OF LIFE

How often do you stop to think

about the miracle of life?

Touch, taste, feel the world around you.

Look broadly. Breathe deeply.

God gave you so many ways

to experience His marvelous creation!

Take time to use all your senses.

Take time each day to thank Him

just for giving you life.

Lord, bring me to a higher appreciation
of Your world.

Amen

Eden is that old-fashioned house we dwell in every day
without suspecting our abode until we drive away.
Emily Dickinson

The LORD God formed man of the dust
of the ground, and breathed into his nostrils
the breath of life; and man became a living soul.
Genesis 2:7

Every house is builded by some man;
but he that built all things is God.
Hebrews 3:4

O taste and see that the LORD is good:
blessed is the man that trusteth in him.
Psalm 34:8

Earth's crammed with heaven.
Elizabeth Barrett Browning

The earth is full of the goodness of the LORD.
Psalm 33:5

To me every hour of the light and dark
is a miracle, every cubic inch of space
is a miracle.
Walt Whitman

Dear God,

I pray that my daughter
would embrace a simple life...
a life of faithfulness
to You, her family, her friends...
a life unencumbered
by an excess of things,
but rich and full
with laughter, joy, and love.
Amen

GENUINE LIFE

To lead a full life, a life rich in fun,

enjoyment, and good memories,

clear out whatever slows you down.

Relieve yourself of things that burden

you with debt, and focus on what gives

real satisfaction and long–lasting joy.

Don't substitute the illusion of

"having it all" for the genuine joy of living!

Lord, turn my heart to value true riches.

Amen

*A Daughter
Is a Blessing
Forever!*